Praise for *TKO* Series

"Dave Anderson's TKO series is a genuine knockout! The fast flowing format combined with high impact-content ensures that readers in any business and in any country will benefit from the universally sound principles presented."

—Sir Peter Vardy, former chairman and CEO of Reg Vardy PLC

"Leadership guru Dave Anderson's new TKO series guides you through the most important management moments in an innovative, down-to-earth, and short format. These highly readable, action-packed guides bring Anderson's insights straight into your world, usable from the CEO to the newest trainee."

—James Strock, author, *Theodore Roosevelt on Leadership*

"Want to go the distance and be a champion? Let Dave Anderson add power to your punch. The TKO series is loaded with hard-hitting strategies that will knock your competition out of contention."

—Randy Pennington, author, *Results Rule!: Build a Culture that Blows the Competition Away!*

"Don't be fooled by the slim size of Dave Anderson's TKO series books—they each pack a knockout punch. Forget sales and management theory, these bantamweight books hit right at the gut of your business—what you must to do succeed. Quick reads—and if applied, they'll provide you with life-long results."

—Paul McCord, author, *How to Build a Million Dollar Sales Income through Referrals*

TKO
MANAGEMENT!

TEN KNOCKOUT STRATEGIES

for

Becoming the Manager Your People Deserve

DAVE ANDERSON

John Wiley & Sons, Inc.

Published by John Wiley & Sons, Inc., Hoboken, New Jersey.
Published simultaneously in Canada.

Wiley Bicentennial Logo: Richard J. Pacifico

For general information on our other products and services or for technical support, please contact our Customer Care Department within the United States at (800) 762-2974, outside the United States at (317) 572-3993, or fax (317) 572-4002.

Wiley also publishes its books in a variety of electronic formats. Some content that appears in print may not be available in electronic books. For more information about Wiley products, visit our web site at www.wiley.com.

Library of Congress Cataloging-in-Publication Data:

Anderson, Dave, 1961-
    TKO management! : Ten knockout strategies for becoming the manager your people deserve / Dave Anderson.
        p. cm.
    ISBN 978-0-470-17177-6 (pbk.)
    1. Management. 2. Executive ability. 3. Leadership. 4. Organizational effectiveness.
I. Title.
    HD31.A548 2007
    658.4–dc22

                                                            2007012409

Printed in the United States of America
10 9 8 7 6 5 4 3 2 1

Contents

Contents

Acknowledgments

Many thanks to my wife, Rhonda, who runs our business, covers my back, and keeps it all together as I jet around the world acting like I have a "real" job. Thanks also to the outstanding support staff and work partners in our California, Texas, and Virginia offices. You're my very own dream team.

About the Author

Dave Anderson is president of LearnToLead, an international sales and leadership training organization. Dave has authored nine books, including the Wiley titles, *Up Your Business, If You Don't Make Waves You'll Drown,* and *How to Deal with Difficult Customers.* He gives over 100 seminars and keynote speeches internationally each year and writes leadership columns for two national magazines. His web site, www.learntolead.com, has tens of thousands of subscribers in forty countries that enjoy an archive of over 400 free training articles. To inquire about having Dave speak to your group contact his Agoura Hills, California office at 800-519-8224 or 818-735-9503 (Intl). Dave is a member of the National Speaker's Association.

Introduction

With today's pace of business and as thin as you're spread as an employee, spouse, parent, and friend, you need high-impact information on how to improve your skills and elevate your organization—and you need it fast, without the hype, void of academics and lacking complexity. This management edition of Wiley's TKO series is the answer.

This book has ten short Rounds that all get to the point and are filled with meaty strategies you can apply right away. In each chapter you'll find Right Hook Rules quotes and sound bites that reinforce what you're learning. You'll also relate to the TKO Tales that take true-life situations and use them as a context for how the principles you're learning can be applied for greater results. If you're looking for an academic recipe for getting better as a manager you won't find it in *TKO Management*. But you will find no-nonsense, in-the-trenches strategies that work in the real-world management arena. Finally, throughout each Round you'll find key Left Jab Laws that will be the catalysts to turning this book into a change agent for your business.

Each Round in *TKO Management* concludes with a series of action-oriented Standing Eight Count Questions and the book finishes up with a bullet-point summary of each Round's key points for quick reference and review. It's the *Cliff Notes* version of the manuscript and I encourage you to refer to it over again as you convert the process of becoming a better manager from a fast reading of this book into a process of continual improvement.

A few words of caution on the TKO series: while the strategies presented in this book are not academic and easy to apply, they're still hard work. Nonetheless, anything worthwhile is worth breaking a sweat for, and the TKO format will make the hard work you have ahead of you more doable, enjoyable, and rewarding.

ROUND 1

Look in the Mirror

Let's Start with Tough Talk

One of the biggest mistakes managers make is running around all day trying to improve everyone who is working for them. They say things like, "if we could just get these people better—get them more serious and committed to success—then everything would be all right." But the fact is that nothing gets better in your organization measurably or sustainably until the managers themselves improve. Training and improving everyone around the managers is important; but that amounts to hacking at the leaves of what it takes to improve an organization, whereas developing managers into better leaders is truly striking at the root. Suffice it to say that, in order to become the manager your people deserve, you must continue to work as hard on yourself as you work on your job. In the words of Jim Rohn, "The business gets better when you get better. Never wish it were easier, wish you were better!" Reading and applying what is in this book is your next step in attaining that goal.

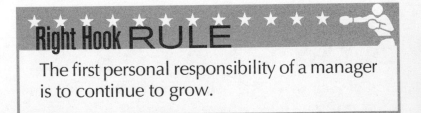

Right Hook RULE

The first personal responsibility of a manager is to continue to grow.

Many managers today live in denial. Rather than look in the mirror and face their own shortfalls and responsibilities, they look out the window and sink into the blame game to try and explain away their lack of greater success. It's become too easy to fault the economy; the competition; the rising interest rates and fuel prices; world conditions; the weather; the time of year; and the list goes on and on. Normally, it is the factors one cannot control that dominate a manager's scapegoat list. The problem is that these uncontrollable issues take your focus, energy, and resources away from the things you can actually do something about! It goes back to the good old 80/20 rule, which tells us that 80 percent of what holds us back from greater results is within our control, while 20 percent is not. Certainly there are things beyond your control that negatively impact your results, but the activities most necessary for greater success are the ones you can do something about. Even in the toughest of times there is a lot you can control: your attitude; work ethic; level of discipline; character choices; where you spend your time and with whom you spend it; who can join the team and who has to leave it. Most would agree that if you spend more time on these controllable factors then the outside conditions won't be as relevant. Or, to put it less delicately, it's helpful to remember the well-known business law, "A fish rots at the head." In other words, when things aren't going well in an operation, or if they are falling short in some area, you don't try to fix matters at the bottom of the hierarchy or in the middle of an organization—or by looking out the window for help. Nope, a fish rots at the head. Quite frankly, it starts to stink at the top first. This, of course, indicts the management of an organization, and that is just as it should be.

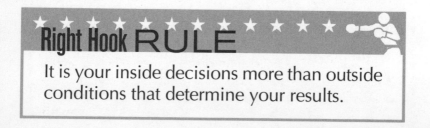

Right Hook RULE

It is your inside decisions more than outside conditions that determine your results.

TKO Tale

Failure in My First Management Position

I made my business mark in the retail automotive field, but I got off to a rough start. My first manager was a corporate terrorist. He micromanaged and was abusive to salespeople and customers alike. He created a lot of stress through intimidation, and I'm embarrassed to say that when I was promoted into my first management job I was just like him. I was a control freak who had to make every decision, have every idea, and solve all the problems. I managed by intimidation and suffered high employee turnover in my department. Because of my micromanaging tendencies I was the "one-man show" and never built a team. In fact, I made my people so dependent on me that when I was off for the day they were immobilized and mostly worthless. As a result, our success was mediocre at best. But to make matters worse, I blamed the team for the lack of success! I wasn't yet aware of the "fish rots at the head" law. I was so busy looking out the window at my "lousy" team that I failed to look in the mirror and evaluate my own ineffectiveness at getting things done through people and by earning significant results.

While I wasn't good at all with the people-work part of my job, I was very good at the paperwork part. I could close deals; I was effective with budgets and forecasts and had a solid grasp of inventory systems and the like. You see, I excelled at the technical part of my job—the tangible portion—the management function, but I didn't know anything about leadership. In fact, I used to believe that management and leadership were synonymous, and I'm chagrined to discover how many people in the workplace still don't understand the difference between management and leadership or the necessity to develop both skill sets into their own management style. As a result, many companies are severely over-managed and grossly under-led. They are

continued

very heavy on systems, controls, forecasting, and budgets and not nearly focused enough on building the human capital within an enterprise or creating an inspiring direction for the organization to progress toward. On the other hand, if you can recall the Internet boom and bust of the late 1990s then you are aware of the problem with having great vision and inspiration, but no real business plan, products, or prospects.

After 18 months in a management position without any type of training, I finally began to learn about the importance of developing both my management and leadership skills—and it opened my eyes to a much more productive way of running businesses. I will always be grateful to the pastor of my church, who stopped by my office one day with a couple of tapes on how to develop leadership skills, because it was the jolt I needed to realize that I was the problem. I regret that it took so long to see the light and I sometimes wish I could go back and find the first group of people I ever managed and apologize; although I suspect many may still be in therapy!

Right Hook RULE

Management and leadership skills can be cultivated and developed. You can improve both aspects with awareness, discipline, and consistent right action.

The best managers accept the fact that to improve their organization, they must first improve themselves. That being

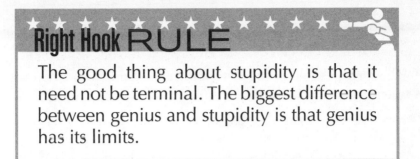

Right Hook RULE

The good thing about stupidity is that it need not be terminal. The biggest difference between genius and stupidity is that genius has its limits.

said, it would be a great time to look in the mirror and evaluate your own management mindset in the areas discussed in the following Left Jab Laws and resolve to make the necessary adjustments to improve your effectiveness. High-impact managers understand the importance of always working on their own skills and style. They are aware of the areas they need to tighten up, toughen up, and loosen up as well. To improve your team you must first improve yourself. As Tolstoy wrote, "Everyone thinks of changing the world but no one thinks of changing him or herself."

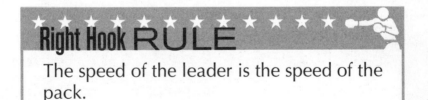

Right Hook RULE

The speed of the leader is the speed of the pack.

Left Jab Laws

1. If your team is mediocre it is probably because you are mediocre. Like begets like.
2. If you're not continually upgrading your own leadership skills then you have zero credibility in advising others on

what it takes to grow. After all, how can you export what you don't have? How can you take people on a journey that you've never been on?

3. Blaming is one of the lowest energy exercises that you can engage in. Blame is the antifocus.

4. Until you diagnose what is truly holding your team back, which in most cases is a lack of more highly developed management and leadership skills on your part, you will continue to prescribe and apply the wrong solutions to remedy the problem.

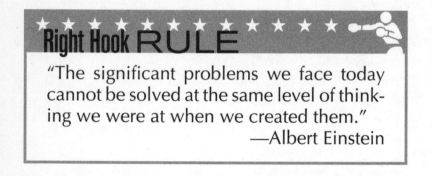

★ ★ ★ ★ ★ ★ ★ ★ ★ ★ ★ ★ ★ ★
Right Hook RULE

"The significant problems we face today cannot be solved at the same level of thinking we were at when we created them."
—Albert Einstein

Standing Eight-Count Questions

1. What is your plan for personal growth?
2. What is the last book you read or CD or DVD you completed that had relevance to improving your skills as a manager?
3. Rate your team from 1 to 10, with 10 as the highest. What does the answer say about you?
4. Which outside condition have you been most prone to blame for your lack of greater success?
5. Which factor that you can control must you spend more time on?
6. Which factor that you can control have you done a good job attending to?
7. What is meant by "a fish rots at the head"?
8. Can you specifically list the three key areas you're better at as a manager today than you were 1 year ago?

Notes

ROUND 2

Understand the Truth about Titles

Opening Bell

I was recently asked a great question in a business talk-radio interview as I discussed my book, *If You Don't Make Waves, You'll Drown:* "Dave, what is the biggest problem that you see with managers today?" I replied, "In my opinion, the biggest problem with managers today is that they don't lead. In fact, one of the most dangerous situations for many organizations today is the high number of men and women in management positions who are not leaders. Instead, they tweak; tinker and tamper; they massage and maintain; they administer and preside but they don't impact followers; they're reluctant to hold others accountable; they fail at creating vision for their organization. Yes, as strange as it sounds, the biggest problem with people carrying around management monikers is that they don't lead! They have a title but they impact no one and add little value to their organization overall."

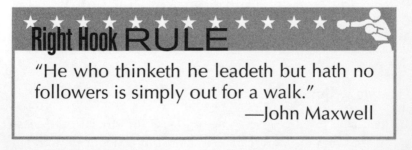

Right Hook RULE

"He who thinketh he leadeth but hath no followers is simply out for a walk."
—John Maxwell

Left Jab Laws

1. While I use the terms *manager* and *leader* as synonyms in this book, what you call the position is not as important as is performing it well.
2. Good management is best defined by performance and not position. It is a choice you make not a place you sit.
3. As a manager, you don't automatically have followers; you only have subordinates. How you act as a manager determines whether or not subordinates ever turn into followers.
4. If your people are not excited about you they won't be excited about where you're trying to take them. Author John Maxwell refers to this as the law of buy-in. In simplest terms, people must buy into your character, competence, and consistency before they buy into your leadership—and you have to do the selling. You accomplish this through your daily words and deeds and ultimately by the results you attain.

★ ★ ★ ★ ★ ★ ★ ★ ★ ★ ★ ★ ★ ★ ★

Right Hook RULE

A title doesn't make you a manager or a leader. All a title does is buy you time to become a leader. What a foolish notion it is for you to believe you've been somehow made more competent by virtue of a change in title!

Leading without a Title

Incidentally, just because someone lacks an official title doesn't mean that they're not a leader. Leadership is about performance and influence and one can demonstrate those traits whether he or she is mopping floors, washing cars, or answering phones. In fact, some of the greatest leaders in recent memory influenced millions of followers, cast exciting visions, and brought forth major change without either a title or any official power! Martin Luther King, Jr., Nelson Mandela, Mahatma Gandhi, and Mother Teresa are just a few examples of the fact that while a title doesn't make you a leader, the lack of a title doesn't preclude you from demonstrating leadership and making a significant impact.

Some manager-wannabes with lofty positions but who leave in their wake a track record void of performance may argue that the authority they have makes them a leader. Wrong! Authority doesn't make anyone a leader. A prison guard has authority; it doesn't mean he's a leader. A policeman, a judge, a teacher, and an usher at the movie theater all have authority but that aspect of their lives certainly doesn't ordain them as leaders.

It Is Your Job to Serve and Not to Wait to Be Served

Whenever I would prepare to promote someone into management I would inform him or her of the Left Jab Laws listed on page 8. It was a humbling experience for many people who had the mistaken notion that management was more about perks and privilege than it was about being an awesome responsibility. Many pretenders with titles spend a lot of time in their offices polishing a chair with their backsides as they wait to be served by their people. This is certainly a corrupt understanding of good management. Effective leaders know that it is their job to serve and support their people; not the other way around. In fact, you need your people more than they need you and I highly recommend that you not forget it. This reality is humbling, but most managers could benefit from a dose of humility from time to time. After all, humility doesn't mean that you think less of yourself. It simply indicates that you think of yourself less.

Right Hook RULE

You're not the Center of the Universe. Sorry, but that job has already been taken.

Equal Application for Rookie and Veteran Managers Alike

While I mentioned that I give the "a title doesn't make you a leader" speech to people new to management, I have found that many veteran leaders need to be reminded of this as well. In fact, if you don't understand the truth about overrated titles versus real performance, you may very well wind up as an expendable figurehead rather than a catalyst that truly makes a difference in the lives of people and in the performance of your organization. Some of you may be at this point now. Others of you may be getting close. In either case, you can turn things around by changing your attitude toward yourself and others. And if you do understand and embrace this principle, then consider this short section as validation of your right beliefs and be encouraged to keep proceeding in a like manner. In the words of Will Rogers, "Even if you're on the right track, you'll get run over if you just sit there!"

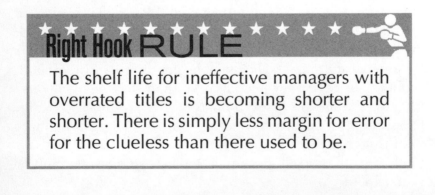

Right Hook RULE

The shelf life for ineffective managers with overrated titles is becoming shorter and shorter. There is simply less margin for error for the clueless than there used to be.

Standing Eight-Count Questions

1. What did I identify as the greatest problem with managers today?
2. What does a title buy you?
3. Good management is not determined by position but by what?
4. Who in your organization has a title but doesn't have a high level of influence?
5. Who in your organization doesn't have an official title but should be considered a leader?
6. What must you personally do to convert any subordinates in your organization into followers?
7. Does the idea of serving others disturb you or make you feel less significant?
8. How do you define the Law of Buy-In?

Notes

R O U N D

Balance Solid Management Skill with Strong Leadership Ability

TKO Tale

As we go into the third Round, allow me to tie key concepts from the past two Rounds together: Look in the mirror and understand the truth about titles. And let me start by relating how I did just the opposite for my first 18 months as an untrained manager. I was a command-and-control type of boss: "My way or the highway. Don't get out of that box and if I want your opinion I'll beat it out of you." I used to walk through the corridors of my business and if I didn't find someone screwing something up, I'd walk through it again. I had an enthusiasm for punishment and I looked for fault like there was a reward for it. If my boss would have let me, I would have built a jail behind our showroom and locked a few people up from time to time. If anyone had asked, I'd have readily claimed to be a strong manager with solid leadership skills. As I look back I am embarrassed. I can now clearly see that I was clueless and naïve, which, with the authority I had as a manager, made me a very dangerous man. As previously admitted, not only did I not look in the mirror, I believed that my management title sanctioned me as a leader. Perhaps you've done the same. Maybe you're doing so now. If so, it's time to stop before it's too late.

How to Excel As a Manager

To excel as a manager it is essential that you face reality about your own leadership style and skills—or lack of skills. One key difference between average and great managers is the word *awareness*. Great managers are far more aware of their own leadership style and the impact it has on others and, thus, can make faster adjustments to improve their style and get back on track if they stray. When they catch themselves overmanaging and underleading, they quickly correct their course. Following are key differences between the functions of management and leadership, broken down in simplest terms, for you to evaluate and determine your own status as a manager who leads well—or not. These points will build perspective that we'll expand on with three key contrasts between overmanaging and leading well.

★ ★ ★ ★ ★ ★ ★ ★ ★ ★ ★ ★ ★
Right Hook RULE

The old command-and-control style of management was stupid 25 years ago, but you could get away with it back then. This is not the case now because we live in the age of the free agent. Employees are more educated, demanding, sensitive, and far more willing to tell you to "stick it" when they decide they've had enough of your abuse.

1. Management is about systems and controls; budgets, structure, scheduling, cost control: it is the technical part of your job that you must perform with excellence. Think of management as the "paperwork" part of your job. Obviously, these are essential aspects of running a successful entity.

2. Leadership is about vision, direction, motivation, and people development. Think of leadership as the "people-work" aspect of your job. Without a balance of these leadership attributes you may become a great historian or scorekeeper, but you won't have a prayer of becoming a great manager.

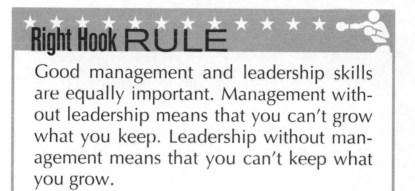

Right Hook RULE

Good management and leadership skills are equally important. Management without leadership means that you can't grow what you keep. Leadership without management means that you can't keep what you grow.

Overmanaged/Underled

Unfortunately, I must submit that in my visits with hundreds of companies and thousands of managers over the years, one of the most disturbing common denominators in the majority of organizations is the tendency of managers to overmanage and underlead. As a natural consequence, most organizations are severely overmanaged and grossly underled. They are very heavy on systems and controls but are not focused nearly enough on people development and are often visionless and void of inspiration. In order to become the manager your people deserve, you'll need to step up and develop a greater degree of leadership ability to compliment your management skills. To offer some perspective on the differences between a management and leadership mindset and to best determine where you may want to make adjustments, consider the following examples while you look straight into the mirror.

Left Jab Laws

1. Managers that lead well spend more time charting the course. Overmanaging causes you to spend more time charting results. What I'm referring to here is the difference between spending your time leading from the front versus sitting in your office and leading from the rear as you polish a chair with your behind.

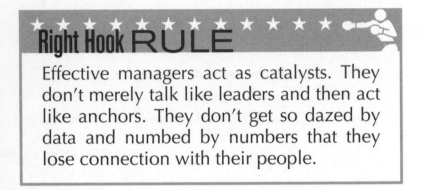

Right Hook RULE

Effective managers act as catalysts. They don't merely talk like leaders and then act like anchors. They don't get so dazed by data and numbed by numbers that they lose connection with their people.

It's important to keep in mind that the front line determines the bottom line. That being said, how much time are you spending at the front line, engaged with your people, listening to customers, and acting as a catalyst?

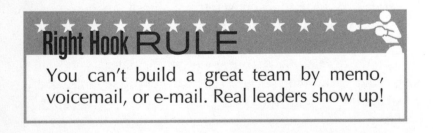

Right Hook RULE

You can't build a great team by memo, voicemail, or e-mail. Real leaders show up!

2. Managers that lead well change before they have to. Overmanaging causes you to pledge allegiance to the status quo. Since a strict management mindset tempts you to

maintain and optimize rather than stretch and innovate, these people are unlikely to change anything until they're backed into a corner and the bottom falls out. Managers with strong leadership skills are much more proactive with change. They lead change, they don't delegate it.

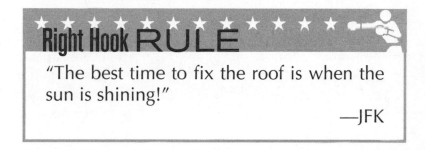

Right Hook RULE

"The best time to fix the roof is when the sun is shining!"

—JFK

The most capable managers act as catalysts because they understand that the longer they study a change and wait for the perfect time to implement it, the less likely they are to ever execute it. They will become immobilized by analysis. Thus, not only are they proactive with change, they are ready, willing, and able to make needed changes more quickly.

Right Hook RULE

"Mister, if you're going to have to swallow a frog, you don't want to stare at that sucker too long! The longer you look at it the uglier it gets."

—Zig Ziglar

3. Managers that lead well understand that it is their responsibility to stretch people and organizations, while overmanaging causes you to maintain people and organizations. This is truly the key difference between how results-producing

managers think and act. It is true that someone in a heavy management mindset is good at maintaining. They will hold things together, keep them humming along, dot every *i* and cross each *t*. But no one in a leadership position is getting paid a dime to maintain a thing. In fact, if you're not stretching, you're not leading.

Just so you're clear as to what I mean by stretching people, here are a few examples: Stretching people means that your expectations are high enough; that you give honest feedback on performance; it says that you hold others accountable for results, and give them additional responsibilities that help them grow.

★ ★ ★ ★ ★ ★ ★ ★ ★ ★ ★ ★ ★ ★ ★
Right Hook RULE

Maintainers in business are a dime a dozen. They're easy to find and cheap to keep. But leaders who can impact others and leave them better than they found them are worth their weight in gold.

Standing Eight-Count Questions

1. How would you define the main differences between management and leadership skills?

2. Do you spend more time charting results or charting the course?

3. Are you more prone to defend the status quo or to change before you have to?

4. In recent months, have you spent more time maintaining your people or have you stretched them?

5. What change have you put off too long? Are you ready to "swallow the frog"?

6. In what areas are the managers you work with overmanaging and underleading? Are you in a position to make them aware of this?

7. Would you rate your own management style overall as more of a coach or of a cop?

8. Are there areas where you tend to overlead and undermanage?

Notes

Create a Winning Workplace Environment

Opening Bell

Abraham Lincoln is one of my favorite leaders to study for lessons I can apply personally and teach to others. Lincoln was a very proactive leader who led from the front—even in the midst of the Civil War. He visited numerous generals on the battlefields and even came under fire while visiting Ft. Stevens in Silver Spring, Maryland as the Confederate general Jubal Early's troops closed within five miles of Washington, D.C. Lincoln also had a reputation for giving his generals clear direction and full support, and then got out of their way. However, he would also replace generals unwilling to lead from the front and who failed to have a bias for action and to act as a catalyst. He once said about General John C. Fremont while explaining his decision to remove him from command in Missouri: "His cardinal mistake is that he isolates himself, and allows nobody to see him, and by which he does not know what is going on in the very matter he is dealing with." Naturally, a key to creating the right environment in your workplace will require that you are a manager who actually shows up and acts as a catalyst and doesn't become isolated or out of touch!

Right Hook RULE

The Oxford Dictionary's definition of lead: Guiding or showing the way. Going in front.

Environment Dictates Behavior

The health and vitality of your workplace environment is paramount and it requires diligence. Think of it as a garden. It requires constant attention: weeding, seeding, and planting so you can harvest results. If you stop paying attention to your garden for long, the weeds will take it over. The same holds true for your environment. As Winston Churchill warned, "When the eagles are silent the parrots will jabber." And while every team member in an organization contributes to either the health or demise of your environment, as a manager it is your responsibility to set the tone and create an atmosphere in which people remain ultimately effective and the right things get consistently done. The tone you set will determine whether people feel administered or led—whether they feel like personnel or people. In fact, whatever your environment feels like on a daily basis— the degree of urgency, level of energy, and evidence of team work—is a reflection of you. Remember Round one: Look in the mirror; a fish rots at the head.

Many managers don't pay nearly enough attention to their environments because, as indicated in the last Round, they spend more time leading from their offices than leading from the front. This is a significant management fault because of the following seven words: environment dictates behavior and behaviors determine results. Ponder that statement for a moment because it has profound implications for your organization. *Environment dictates behavior and behavior determines results.* For instance, if you go to a church, people behave a certain way there because of the environment. The same can be said for a library, a museum, a nightclub, or a ballgame. Based on this fact, consider the following: If people behave in accordance with the environment in which they find themselves and you want to improve their behaviors, you must change the environment in which they work first! In fact, one of the most common mistakes managers make is trying to change or improve people's behaviors without changing or improving the environment in which those behaviors are found, and they quickly discover that the changes they're looking for never stick. They might last a couple hours or maybe for a few days at the most.

Right Hook RULE

Competent managers should act as thermostats and not as thermometers. Thermostats are active; they create the feel and set the temperature for the environment. Thermometers, on the other hand, are reactive. They respond to whatever happens to be going on around them.

—John Maxwell

Following are four steps to help you create a winning environment in your department and in your organization overall. These aren't the only steps you can take, but they'll go a long way in creating the conditions for the changed behaviors that will elevate your results.

1. Become more visible and accessible by leading from the front of your organization.

Building on the example from Lincoln, this is perhaps the most essential step to acting as a thermostat in your organization.

Leading from the front doesn't mean that you have to literally go out and stand at the front of your workplace, although that may be helpful from time to time in order to see for yourself what is taking place. Leading from the front does require that you stay connected to your people; engaging them with questions; giving them feedback; offering positive reinforcement; keeping the vision at the forefront of their minds; and holding them accountable. Needless to say, this is difficult to accomplish if you're in the habit of roosting in your office, collecting more calluses on your backside than on your hands or feet, because I can assure you that you cannot build a great team by remote control.

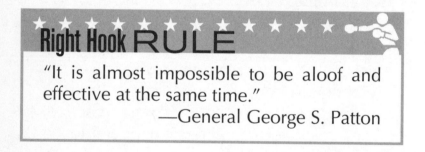

Right Hook RULE

"It is almost impossible to be aloof and effective at the same time."
—General George S. Patton

One method for becoming more visible and accessible is to commit to daily "wander-arounds," where you deliberately get out of your office and wander around connecting with people, taking their questions, listening to their ideas, and getting involved with customers. However, if you're having a bad day and your attitude is off track, please don't feel the need to make yourself more visible or else your wander-around may turn into a drive-by! Frankly, part of being an effective manager is recognizing when you're having a lousy day and are projecting a sour disposition and to limit the damage that you do.

TKO Tale

A manager who attended one of my seminars had such a strong habit of staying in his office all day and rarely engaging his people that he actually scheduled his wander-arounds. He'd make appointments with himself twice a day to remind him to get out and actually lead rather than simply preside. He told me that he realized that the environment in his workplace was going to be created in his department with or without him and that if he didn't step up and set the tone, someone else would. And that someone else was normally the employee with personal problems, a negative attitude, or a chip on his shoulder the size of a lumber yard.

---

2. Establish a high set of expectations.
When the bar is set high in your organization, it will change the way the workplace feels. There will be more focus, urgency, and second-effort performances. But when people are allowed to simply go through the motions, it can put your culture into a coma. Face it: It's a lot tougher for people to loll or drift when there is a lot expected and when you've created a culture of accountability.

3. Provide vision and shared purpose.
A vision is a precise and bold picture of where you're headed as an organization and helps to inspire and unite the team toward a common end. Shared purpose is the meaning created when the team is involved in a cause much larger than any individual—a destination they could never hope to end up at on their own. Quite frankly, vision-driven organizations feel different. There is more purpose, urgency, enthusiasm, and teamwork. Vision will be covered in greater depth in Round seven. For now, here are a handful of thoughts to help refine and expand your understanding of what corporate vision is.

Left Jab Laws

1. Vision is a specific direction. In business, it is best if this destination is quantifiable. You must be able to track and measure your progress and results.

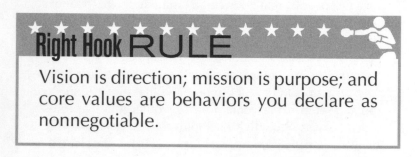

Right Hook RULE

Vision is direction; mission is purpose; and core values are behaviors you declare as nonnegotiable.

2. Vision must bring various departments together in a common cause. Each entity must understand its own role in the vision.

3. Lock like a laser on your vision but don't become attached to how you get there. Remain focused without losing flexibility.

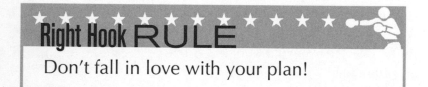

Right Hook RULE

Don't fall in love with your plan!

4. Vision must start with the leadership of an organization.

Right Hook RULE

"Just as no great painting was ever designed by committee; no outstanding vision has ever emerged from the herd."
— Warren Bennis

TKO Tale

In 1954, Florence Chadwick, one of the best swimmers in the world, decided to attempt the 23 mile swim from Catalina Island to the California coast in spite of foggy, drizzly, inclement weather. Fifteen hours into the swim, Chadwick was disoriented, exhausted, and wanted to give up, but her support team in the accompanying watercraft encouraged her telling her that she was doing great and was closer than she realized. After some additional effort, Florence gave up and was taken to shore. In an interview afterwards Chadwick remarked that once the boat took her to shore she was startled to see how close she actually was to the shoreline and that if she could have seen the destination she wouldn't have given up; but it was covered in fog due to the weather.

The same can be said for your people in the workplace. If their destination is not clear, if it is covered in fog, it's easier to become indifferent, apathetic, and to throw in the towel. If you desire more teamwork, focus, and purpose as part of your workplace environment then it is essential that you perform one of the first responsibilities of anyone in a management position: to define what the future will look like; to line people up with that vision; and inspire them to make it in spite of obstacles.

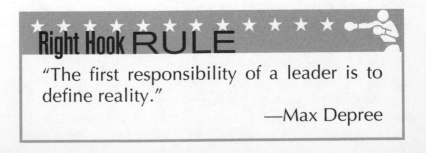

Right Hook RULE

"The first responsibility of a leader is to define reality."
—Max Depree

4. Publicly control your attitude and emotions.

It should be a fair expectation that as one rises higher on the leadership ladder, that he or she is more responsible for publicly controlling his or her emotions. This is made even more important when you realize that there is little in the workplace that shoots a hole through the fabric of a winning environment more than a leader with a bad attitude. Or one who is a pessimist, a whiner, a complainer, a gossip, the constant critic, one who sobs about personal problems, or who is just a dyed-in-the-wool wimp.

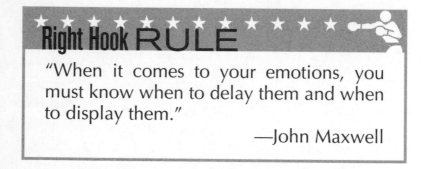

Right Hook RULE

"When it comes to your emotions, you must know when to delay them and when to display them."

—John Maxwell

When followers engage in gossip, bring their personal problems to work, or whine and complain, major distractions emerge and severe damage is inflicted on a healthy workplace environment. But when a manager engages in this nonsense, the negative impact is far more devastating than when a follower behaves poorly, because there is more at stake. What you must understand as the leader of your people is that by virtue of your position, you are on display. Your people see everything you do and hear all that you say and whether good or bad, negative or positive, it will be magnified many times over. If you're not comfortable with that sort of scrutiny then get out of management because it comes with the territory. After all, to whom much is given, much is required.

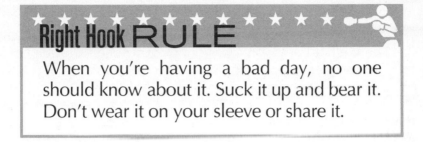

Right Hook RULE

When you're having a bad day, no one should know about it. Suck it up and bear it. Don't wear it on your sleeve or share it.

A manager at a seminar approached me during a break and told me that he disagreed with my statement that it is unwise for a leader to discuss personal problems with followers. He remarked that he did it frequently because it helped him build rapport and it showed his team that he was a real person just like they were. I suggested that what he was doing was irresponsible because it would distract his people by taking their eyes of their jobs and putting them on his problem. Furthermore, I remarked that this practice would diminish his credibility and cheapen his presence as a manager. I told him that as harsh at it may sound I was fairly certain that 90 percent of his people didn't care about his problems and the other 10 percent were glad he had them, so there was little to gain by publicly discussing them!

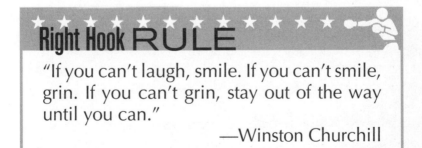

Right Hook RULE

"If you can't laugh, smile. If you can't smile, grin. If you can't grin, stay out of the way until you can."
—Winston Churchill

Left Jab Laws

1. Realize that your problems aren't your problems. It's how you respond to them that makes it a problem. At the outset

it was just a condition of being in business. An improper reaction normally turns it into a problem.

2. You are not born with a good or bad attitude. Attitude is a choice! Before you make the wrong choice, keep the big picture in mind: the impact your actions will have on others and the environment where they work.

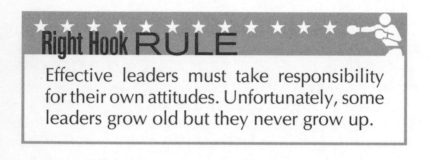

Right Hook RULE

Effective leaders must take responsibility for their own attitudes. Unfortunately, some leaders grow old but they never grow up.

3. If things are not going well in your current position, keep in mind that what you most likely need is a change of self and not a change of scene.

4. When you make a mistake, admit it quickly. This is the sign of a good attitude and will teach your followers to emulate your positive example. I suggest that you do not emulate the Duke of Wellington who once haughtily drew himself up to his full height and thundered to one of his staff officers, "God knows I have many faults, but being wrong is not one of them!"

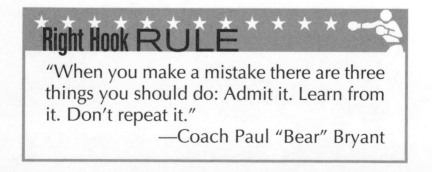

Right Hook RULE

"When you make a mistake there are three things you should do: Admit it. Learn from it. Don't repeat it."
                    —Coach Paul "Bear" Bryant

5. Give away credit. This builds your credibility, improves the attitude of your team, and teaches them to be unselfish.

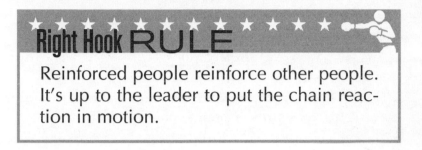

Right Hook RULE

Reinforced people reinforce other people. It's up to the leader to put the chain reaction in motion.

Standing Eight-Count Questions

1. What percentage of the time do you spend isolated in your office versus the time you spend engaged with the people you manage?

2. Do you perform consistent daily wander-arounds?

3. Are your workplace expectations clear enough and high enough?

4. Do you have a clear, quantifiable vision for your team this year? Are you sure? Can your people articulate it?

5. Do you feel that you act as the catalyst—a thermostat—for your environment or do you find yourself spending more time reacting and recording like a thermometer?

6. Which aspect of your attitude must you do a better job of publicly controlling?

7. Have you created a trusting and open environment by admitting your mistakes and by giving away credit whenever it is due?

8. Which of the tips for creating a winning environment must you commit more time to so that you can create the environment that produces the results you're looking for?

Notes

R O U N D

Become a Powerful Motivator

Opening Bell: Motivation by Granddaughter

Two attendees to my management seminar related their frustration at trying to motivate "Bob" to sell more than twelve automobiles per month. Bob retired from the military at a rank that provided a significant monthly benefit check and, thus, was not motivated by dollars. Since eight to ten units per month was the national mean for automobile unit sales per month, Bob was above average and had a great attitude, work ethic, and integrity. However, his managers knew he was capable of selling far more than his monthly dozen but nothing they did to motivate him worked. After hearing me present a motivation principle in class that stressed the importance of customizing your motivational approach to fit the employee by finding his or her hot button rather than try and fit the employee into one's own motivational approach, they decided to return to their business and get a bit more creative in their efforts to get Bob past the mark of twelve.

When the managers returned to a seminar the following year for a refresher they told me that they had determined that Bob's motivational "hot button" was his two granddaughters. He bragged about them constantly and had pictures of them proudly displayed in his office. They decided to make Bob a special incentive deal for the month and promised him that they'd buy each granddaughter a $25.00 savings bond for each car over twelve that he sold that month. The result? Bob delivered twenty-five cars that month! In fact, the managers have kept the special incentive in place for Bob—he doesn't participate in the other incentive programs the dealership offers during the month—and he has never sold fewer than twenty since. I think we could agree that Bob didn't all of a sudden get that much better. He always had the ability within him. It just took a couple of managers with the right approach to draw it out.

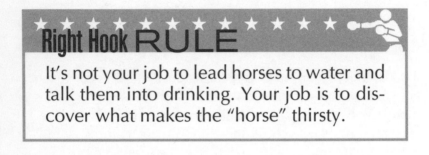

Right Hook RULE

It's not your job to lead horses to water and talk them into drinking. Your job is to discover what makes the "horse" thirsty.

Find Their Hot Buttons

Human capital rarely arrives in your business fully developed. It is up to you as a manager to bring out the best in your people and develop them through motivation, training, and coaching. Of course, it is essential that you hire the right person to begin with. After all, an employee must give you something to work with. For help with hiring, read the book *TKO Hiring* in the Wiley TKO series. After all, an employee must give you drive, attitude, character, talent, and energy to work with before you can develop him or her to higher levels.

To develop the people you manage you'll need to learn what makes each person tick; train them in a manner that leverages their strengths and minimizes their weaknesses and coach them with the feedback and accountability they need to stay on track and develop productive habits and routines. This Round will cover the motivational aspects of development and Round six will provide you with the tools to train and coach your team.

Right Hook RULE

A manager's job is to take the human capital they've been entrusted with and make it more valuable tomorrow than it is today.

Left Jab Laws

Here are six steps to help you become a more powerful motivator:

1. Create an environment that is motivating.

This includes eliminating the following demotivators that will break your people's momentum. While what follows is not a complete list of potential demotivators, you're likely to recognize quite a few of them.

- Unclear expectations
- Poor training procedures
- No latitude or discretion
- Too many or unproductive meetings
- Micromanagement
- Tolerating poor performers
- No clear vision
- Meaningless work
- No positive reinforcement or recognition
- Negative superiors
- Poor communication; not being "let in" on things
- Negative coworkers
- No room to advance
- Dishonest leaders or coworkers
- Lack of trust from management
- Flavor-of-the-month programs with no follow-up

- Management that doesn't listen to ideas
- Unhealthy internal competition

You can certainly add other demotivators to this list, but the issues listed are a pretty good place to start. Think of your workplace as a minefield and the demotivators listed here as the landmines. As long as you allow the landmines to remain in the environment, your people may be pumped up for a while, but before long, they'll step on one of the "mines" and get blown up. You may never be able to rid your environment of all these aspects simultaneously, but you've got to stay after it. It takes constant effort and attention.

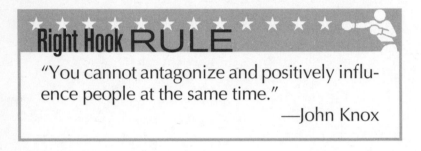

★ ★ ★ ★ ★ ★ ★ ★ ★ ★ ★ ★ ★
Right Hook RULE

"You cannot antagonize and positively influence people at the same time."
—John Knox

2. Address internal motivational needs.

Without a doubt, external motivators like money, prizes, and other tangible goodies are motivators. However, if you peruse surveys employees take on what means the most to them in the workplace you won't find money at the top of the list. I'm not trying to diminish the importance of money, I am merely pointing out that if certain internal motivational triggers are not satisfied, then the external motivators you throw at people will not move them very far or for long.

Following is a list of common internal motivators that regularly show up on employee feedback surveys as being most essential to them on the job. Determine how well you address these factors as a leader and decide where you must do better in order to get the most out of your people:

- Being able to make a difference
- Recognition for a job well done

- Being part of a special team
- Being part of a special cause
- Being trusted with decisions and resources
- The opportunity to grow personally
- The sense of ownership that comes with being let in on things

Right Hook RULE

Money may buy employees' hands but it is the internal motivational factors that win their heads and hearts. You're paying for all three. It's your job to be sure you're getting them.

3. Customize your motivational approach to fit each individual on your team.

If you need further proof, re-read the story of "Savings Bond Bob" at the beginning of this section. And if you're not sure what motivates your employees, ask them!

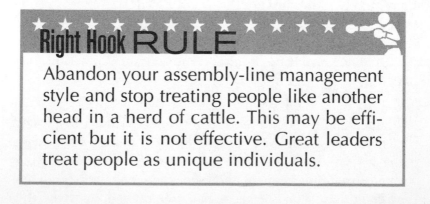

Right Hook RULE

Abandon your assembly-line management style and stop treating people like another head in a herd of cattle. This may be efficient but it is not effective. Great leaders treat people as unique individuals.

4. Remember that motivations change over time.
It's your job as a leader to maintain a strong enough relationship with your people to ensure that you're pressing the buttons that mean the most to them.

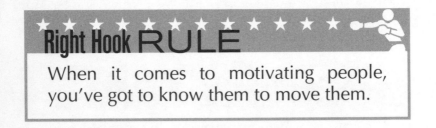

Right Hook RULE

When it comes to motivating people, you've got to know them to move them.

5. You, as an example.
If your words and deeds match, you will motivate your people by building trust and credibility. However, if you talk right and walk left, you'll leave your people behind. Having integrity as a manager means that you do what you said you'd do, when you said you'd do it, and how you said you'd do it.

Right Hook RULE

"As I grow older, I pay less attention to what men say, and instead watch what they do."
                                        —Andrew Carnegie

6. Increase positive reinforcement.
A law of behavioral science teaches that behaviors that get reinforced and rewarded tend to get repeated. This being said, how often do you let your people know about it when they're doing a great job? If you're like too many managers, you're stingy with positive reinforcement and focus more on telling them how they could have done better; what they missed, and why they

must step up next time around. This type of management style wears people out and makes them indifferent and apathetic. People start asking themselves, "if nothing is ever going to be good enough, why am I killing myself to get the job done?"

Four Keys to Positive Reinforcement

1. It should be given as fast after the action as possible because delayed consequences are not effective.
2. It should be specific rather than general.
3. Positive reinforcement is in the eyes of the receiver. The type of reinforcement you give must be customized to fit the recipient. It must mean something to the person getting it. It doesn't matter what you think should motivate the person or what motivates you. This is not about you, it's about the employee.
4. In the absence of positive reinforcement, people are forced to focus more on external rewards to find job satisfaction. After all, if they're never going to be told anything positive or recognized for their contributions, then getting more money out of the boss is the only way they can justify in their own minds why they're still on the job. Oftentimes someone will tell me that they never received much reinforcement growing up and don't get much from their boss. A result, they withhold it from others. Well, I'm sorry that your daddy didn't hug you. Truly I am. And I also feel bad that your boss is so clueless as to not grasp this important aspect of developing others. But you must be bigger than they are and do what is right.

Right Hook RULE

Don't duplicate someone else's management flaws into your own style.

Standing Eight-Count Questions

1. Do you know what moves each of your people?
2. Have you focused too much on external rewards as a source for motivating your team?
3. Which of the landmines listed as demotivators is wreaking the most havoc on your team morale at this very moment?
4. Do you give enough positive reinforcement?
5. Do you offer the reinforcement fast enough after the performance? Do you give it in specific or general terms?
6. Do you have any solid performers like "Savings Bond Bob" with whom you can get creative in an effort to draw out their best and bring them to a higher level?
7. How consistent have your words and deeds been in the past?
8. Does your management style fit the definition of integrity offered in this Round?

Notes

Train and Coach Your People to Reach Their Fullest Potential

Opening Bell

More often than you might believe, my office gets calls from potential clients with the same lament, "Business is down so we need to train our people to do a better job." Or, we hear just the opposite when soliciting business, "Business is down so we can't afford to spend anything on training." Both of these comments are clear evidence that just having a management title doesn't guarantee that one's IQ has ascended beyond room temperature. In fact, I've often wondered how people making these types of old-school comments can keep their people sharp enough to compete in today's marketplace. Honestly, they'd be better off to retire to their caves, watch hours of "The Flintstones," listen to their favorite 78's, and let a manager who "gets it" take the helm.

Right Hook RULE

The cost of training pales in comparison to the cost of ignorance.

Seven Simple Strategies

Following are seven high-impact training and coaching strategies to build your team. They are simple but they require a large dose of commitment and discipline from the leader to embed them into your culture. While motivation, as covered in Round five, is essential to bringing the best out of people, it does not take the place of training. Because, despite what you may have heard, attitude is not everything. Attitude is very important. Everything starts with attitude but it is not everything. People still need a higher level of competence. Otherwise, all a great attitude does is make someone more content with their failures!

Right Hook RULE

If people are on the wrong track, they don't need motivation to get them there faster!

Left Jab Laws

1. Time and money must be made available for training. Spare neither. You'll never find time to train your people. You must make the time.
2. A main focus of training should be to become brilliant in the basics.

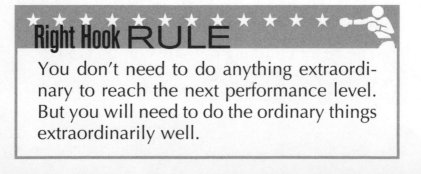

Right Hook RULE

You don't need to do anything extraordinary to reach the next performance level. But you will need to do the ordinary things extraordinarily well.

3. Training meetings get people involved. If a meeting has spectators rather than participants, it is not a real training meeting. Role-play; pass out a fill-in-the-blank handout; have an attendee conduct part of the meeting; watch a training DVD; and so forth.

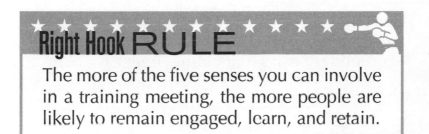

Right Hook RULE

The more of the five senses you can involve in a training meeting, the more people are likely to remain engaged, learn, and retain.

4. End all formal training sessions with marching orders. A marching order is a task that you have your people practice or learn more about in between training meetings: a product of the week; a closing technique of the week; an objection of the week to overcome; and the like.

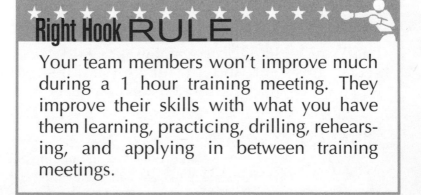

Right Hook RULE

Your team members won't improve much during a 1 hour training meeting. They improve their skills with what you have them learning, practicing, drilling, rehearsing, and applying in between training meetings.

5. Top managers in the company should attend or participate in training whenever possible. This lends credibility to the

meetings and sends the message that what people are doing is important.*

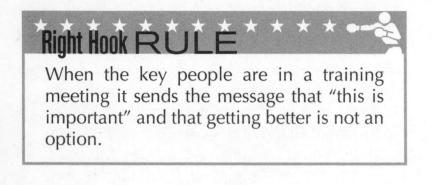

Right Hook RULE

When the key people are in a training meeting it sends the message that "this is important" and that getting better is not an option.

6. Training meetings must be credible. This means you don't cancel them just because they're inconvenient or you're short handed. They are a priority and must be executed without excuse.

Right Hook RULE

Every organization needs a handful of non-negotiable disciplines that get done consistently, without fail and regardless of the cost. Consistent and meaningful training meetings should be one of these vital tasks.

7. Training is a process and not an event. It is an ongoing endeavor. It is not a one-time payment but an installment plan. It must become embedded in your culture in order to develop your people to their fullest potential.

★ ★ ★ ★ ★ ★ ★ ★ ★ ★ ★ ★ ★ ★

Right Hook RULE

If you have good people and you don't invest time and money in them, you don't deserve those people. In fact, you deserve to lose them, and if they do remain in your business you don't deserve great results from them because you're seeking a prize without paying a price.

The Manager As a Coach

Coaching differs from training in that it is more ongoing whereas training is more structured and is more of a step-by-step process. In simplest terms, coaching means that you observe performance, analyze it, and then offer feedback based on what you see. Needless to say, you cannot be an effective coach if you aren't in the trenches to see what is taking place as pointed out in Round three.

Following are some guidelines for coaching people to their fullest potential on the job. I will cover one-on-one coaching sessions extensively in this section because it is your biggest opportunity to positively impact the people working for you.

Left Jab Laws

1. Effective coaching means that you don't simply talk about what good performance looks like. Instead, you must show people what good performance looks like.

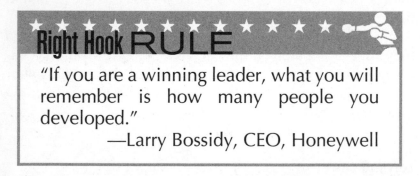

★ ★ ★ ★ ★ ★ ★ ★ ★ ★ ★ ★ ★
Right Hook RULE

People would rather see a sermon than hear one.

2. Since coaching people involves giving them feedback, you must be balanced in your approach. You can accomplish this in a formal one-on-one session or on-the-fly during the day. A combination of both is the most effective approach to impact people. Your feedback should be very soon after the performance, and it must be specific, honest, and constructive.
3. Conduct effective one-on-one coaching sessions.

Since managers are paid to impact people rather than just maintain them, it is essential that you prioritize face-time with your team members in order to engage them, coach, reinforce, and challenge them. However, you'll have far greater success in doing so if you'll follow the five step strategy I present for you in this section.

★ ★ ★ ★ ★ ★ ★ ★ ★ ★ ★ ★ ★
Right Hook RULE

"If you are a winning leader, what you will remember is how many people you developed."
        —Larry Bossidy, CEO, Honeywell

Schedule and conduct the one-on-ones consistently. Conduct them in a completely private setting. Give your employees your undivided attention; don't allow any interruptions or distractions. Your message should be that nothing is more important than this session.

TKO Tale

Early in my management career I attended a training workshop where the instructor admonished us to hold one-on-one coaching sessions with our team members in order to develop them. He said it was one of a manager's biggest responsibilities. Unfortunately, the class I attended was full of "should be's" but short on "how to's." Thus, I returned to my department determined to conduct one-on-ones but without a clue how to do so. As a result, I did the best I could but, ultimately, my one-on-ones were not effective. In fact, they were similar to an indictment. I'd bring in a salesperson, sit him down, and read off a list of ten charges against him: "You did this wrong!", "You fell short in these sixteen areas!", "You really fouled that assignment up!" and the like. Soon, none of my people wanted to have one-on-ones with me and they all became busy when it was time for our visit together. I realized that the instructor had failed to mention that in addition to being one of the potentially highest impact encounters with our people, one-on-one coaching sessions could also become one of the most demoralizing if conducted improperly.

Normally, you will conduct one-on-ones in your office, but you can also create value by going to your employee's office and conducting it there. To paraphrase General Patton, "Don't make your people come to you. You go to them. In that manner they maintain maximum productivity and you get to see what's going on in your operation by getting out and about."

Follow This Five Step Process for One-On-One Coaching:

1. Ask. Ask the employees about their goals or objectives. Get them to identify plan how to achieve them; what, if anything, is holding them back; and what would help them make progress.

Asking is the opposite of how most managers start one-on-ones. Normally, they do all the talking while their employee sits there, eyes glazed over, mentally checking out of the process. Remember, the one-on-one is about your employee. It's not about you! If you want to give speeches, join your local chapter of Toastmasters. In order to effectively develop followers you will need solid two-way communication.

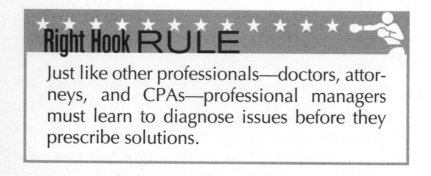

Right Hook RULE

Just like other professionals—doctors, attorneys, and CPAs—professional managers must learn to diagnose issues before they prescribe solutions.

2. Listen. Listen to them without interrupting. Guide and help them discover their own answers.

Guiding and helping them discover their own answers means that, rather than assume the role of Mr. or Ms. "Fix it" for everything that ails your team members, you teach them to become less dependent on you and to learn to think for themselves by asking questions like, "What do you think you should do?", "What is the first step you can take toward making this happen?", "What are the options you're considering?" and so forth. This will also help you glean a clear idea of their states of mind and their abilities, values, and thought process.

These first two steps, asking and listening, will take up three-fourths of your coaching time. You should spend 80 percent of this time listening. Your ability to maintain this balance will greatly determine the level of success you have and the impact you are able to make throughout the remainder of the one-on-one.

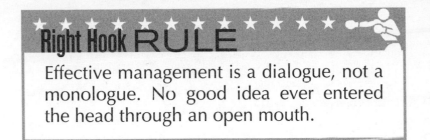

Right Hook RULE

Effective management is a dialogue, not a monologue. No good idea ever entered the head through an open mouth.

3. Coach. Now you're ready to coach the actions your employee needs to take to improve his or her performance. Use this time to talk about problems or areas that need improvement and to suggest strategies to help him or her overcome an obstacle or move toward a goal.

Most managers wrongly begin their one-on-ones with the "coach" step. They begin to prescribe solutions before engaging the employee or listening to what they have to say. This shuts them down and can make them defensive. When you follow the "ask" and "listen" steps first, employees are more open to what you have to say when you reach the "coach" stage because they have had a chance to express themselves and feel understood. Your advice will also have more credibility at this stage than it would if you had started rattling off quick-fix cures to what ails them right from the start.

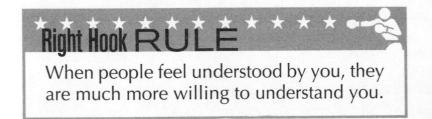

Right Hook RULE

When people feel understood by you, they are much more willing to understand you.

4. Reinforce. While you will give your people plenty of reinforcement for the good works they perform throughout the

day, this stage of the one-on-one offers you the chance to formally point out and acknowledge what they are doing right. Take the time to praise specific behaviors and results. Point out talents, attitudes, and knowledge they have that will help them reach their goals. Affirm them by asserting that you believe they can do it.

Don't give someone praise for something he or she doesn't deserve during the one-on-one. This practice artificially boosts the ego and only serves to reinforce a state of denial as he or she believes that they are doing better than they truly are. But, if someone is doing certain things well and you want to see him or her doing more of those things, then it is essential that you point them out and reinforce them and be as specific as possible when you describe the behavior.

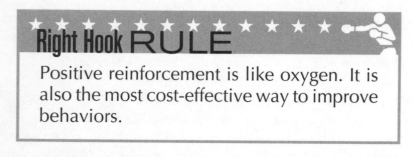

Right Hook RULE

Positive reinforcement is like oxygen. It is also the most cost-effective way to improve behaviors.

5. Challenge. Challenge them to become their best. Ask them to commit to specific actions and time frames. Explain that you will follow up on their progress. Use this step as an opportunity to stretch the employees as well as to hold them accountable for past commitments.

Right Hook RULE

Human beings are a lot like rubber bands. They are the most useful when stretched.

Schedule One-on-Ones

You are unlikely to find time to conduct these important coaching sessions and, since they're too important to leave to chance, I recommend that you schedule them—daily, weekly, or monthly, whichever works best for you.

Right Hook RULE

Don't prioritize your schedule. Instead, schedule your priorities.

Conduct One-on-Ones with Your Top People First

You cannot build a great organization by engaging in endless rescue missions and performing damage control. At the same time, you cannot afford to ignore and take for granted your top people who are giving you the most to work with. Thus, be sure that you are listening to, supporting, coaching, and stretching your best performers as a priority.

Right Hook RULE

It's easier to help someone rise from good to great than it is to elevate one from miserable to mediocre because the good performer gives you a solid foundation to build upon.

Compile a One-on-One Binder

Get organized. Assemble a binder with a section for each person on your one-on-one agenda. Keep notes from what was discussed at your last session; commitments made by the employee that you must follow up on; performance goals; charts; and the like.

Anyone who uses his memory as a filing system chooses a fool as his tool.

Don't Allow the One-on-One to Devolve Into a Therapy Session

Hold up the mirror and help people focus on what they can control and never let them assume the position of victim or martyr. Teach your people that failure is not an accident; they either set themselves up for it or they don't.

When someone chooses a behavior—good or bad—they are also choosing the consequences that come along with that behavior. They are not victims.

Standing Eight-Count Questions

1. Are your training meetings scheduled and adhered to without excuse?

2. Do you get people involved during your training sessions or are they more likely to assume a spectator's role?

3. Are marching orders a part of your training regimen?

4. Do the top people in your department, including you, attend or conduct a portion of the training sessions?

5. Do you and the other managers on your team spend enough time showing people what good performance looks like ... or do you spend more time talking about what good performance should look like?

6. How often do you conduct one-on-ones? In the past, has the tone been mostly constructive or negative?

7. Do you have a one-on-one binder? Do you schedule these sessions?

8. In the past, have you spent more time with your top or bottom performers during one-on-ones?

Notes

ROUND  7

Create a Dynamic Vision and Strategy for Your Organization

In order to set a meaningful vision, leaders must be in tune with the aspirations and goals of their people. Astute managers take the vision from "me" to "we." They engage their people and solicit their input on what it will take to reach the vision because people will support what they help create. But they must weigh in before they buy-in. All of the work involved with creating and communicating a compelling vision is worth the price because vision-driven organizations feel differently. There is more purpose, more meaning, and greater teamwork and urgency because people feel they are part of a cause, a campaign. They no longer merely have "jobs."

TKO Tale

Early in my management career I used to dictate vision and expect everyone to fall into line; after all, I was the boss, right? Perhaps I was the boss but I wasn't much of a leader. As was made clear in Round two, the titles of boss and leader are not synonymous. After dictating my vision I found that followers complied but they never committed; they went as far as they had to, but no further.

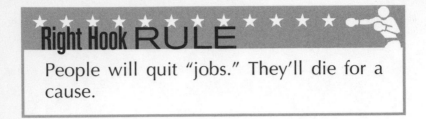

Right Hook RULE

People will quit "jobs." They'll die for a cause.

It's Your Job

There are many things a manager can and should delegate, but creating vision for his or her organization is not one of them. It is the manager's responsibility to define what the future will look like; to line people up with that vision and then to inspire them to make it happen regardless of distractions, setbacks, and other obstacles. Managers create focus through a compelling vision that brings others to a place they've never been before. They manage meaning in the workplace by communicating the vision.

However, it is not desirable or necessary for the manager to devise the entire strategy to reach the vision. To create a strategy that followers take ownership of, you must include them in the process. This Round presents strategies for both creating vision and facilitating strategy.

As you read further about visions, keep in mind that the word *vision* itself is often misunderstood. It is not designed to be some happy hot-tub talk phrase that makes you feel warm and fuzzy while you sing choruses of "Kumbaya." Rather, vision is a specific, quantifiable direction. You can track it and you know for sure when you hit it ... or if you fall short. Think of vision as your overall goal for the year with many smaller goals set up as mile markers along the way. The vision should include a handful—one to three at the most—of the performance components most relevant and important to your enterprise.

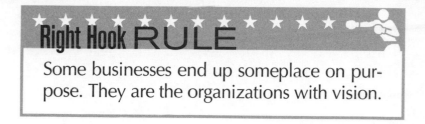

Some businesses end up someplace on purpose. They are the organizations with vision.

Left Jab Laws

1. Your organization's vision should be big enough so that initially you're not quite sure how you'll get there. If you know for sure that you can reach your vision and can see every zig and zag necessary to attain it then it's very likely that your vision isn't big enough. In fact, if it's too easy to see from the starting gate to the finish line you could be limiting yourself from new approaches, creative innovations, and group synergies that provide genuine breakthroughs. After all, visions are not supposed to be "no brainers" or slam dunks. You shouldn't be able to sleepwalk there. Vince Lombardi put it well when he said, "A vision that moves and inspires to new performance levels must be created without reference to the past, without reference to what seems possible at the moment. Otherwise, you'll be prone to limit your vision to what appears to be realistic, and where is the drive, inspiration, and energy in that?"

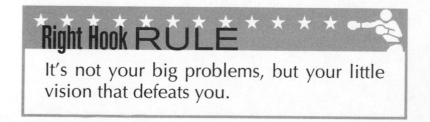

It's not your big problems, but your little vision that defeats you.

2. Your organization's bold vision should make everyone involved feel both excited and uncomfortable. Yes, you

should believe that you can reach it but you shouldn't be able to get there with a business-as-usual approach. Within the context of this tension, you can come up with a breakthrough.

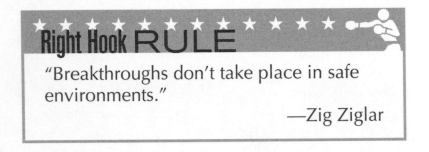

Right Hook RULE

"Breakthroughs don't take place in safe environments."

—Zig Ziglar

3. Your vision should be big enough to cause you to do something today you would not do without the vision. This is always the test to determine if your vision is big enough. If it is not causing you to do something today that you wouldn't be doing without the vision, then your vision is impotent.

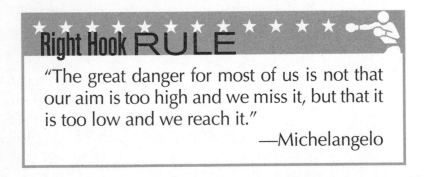

Right Hook RULE

"The great danger for most of us is not that our aim is too high and we miss it, but that it is too low and we reach it."

—Michelangelo

4. Developing a vision progresses in the following order: The leader must first catch it, then cast it, then communicate it constantly until there is genuine commitment from the entire team to reach it.

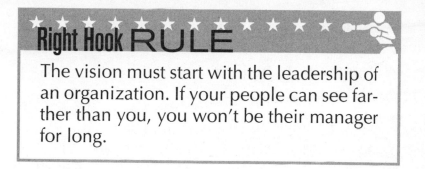

The vision must start with the leadership of an organization. If your people can see farther than you, you won't be their manager for long.

5. When beginning the vision-development process for the organization, it is best to begin with a small number of people and then bring the masses into the process as it takes shape. Ideally, this will be the key leader and/or his or her key leadership team members.

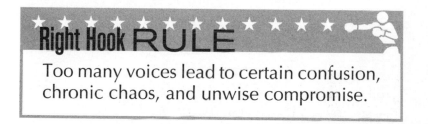

Too many voices lead to certain confusion, chronic chaos, and unwise compromise.

6. Casting your organization's vision means sharing it with people at all levels and showing them where they fit into the picture and what's in it for them—and the whole team—when you get there. This is your chance to get feedback from employees on how to reach the vision and gives them a sense of ownership in the process. You can't "dictate" a vision and expect it to move people. Casting a vision properly takes patience and effective people skills. Have your best communicators impart the vision and initially target the leaders or "unofficial" leaders in each department for their input, buy-in, and support.

Right Hook RULE

You can't do it alone!

7. The vision itself must be easy to understand, uncomplicated, and your people should be able to articulate it in a
   few short sentences. This makes it easier to communicate.
   By communicating the vision constantly, you let people
   know you mean business and that the vision process is not
   the latest flavor of the month.

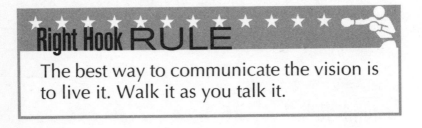

Right Hook RULE

The best way to communicate the vision is
to live it. Walk it as you talk it.

8. Gaining commitment. Only when the previous steps are
   followed can you expect a genuine commitment and enthusiasm toward the organization's vision. It will take some
   time. Be sincere, consistent and passionate about where
   the vision will take you. If you and the other leaders are not
   passionate about the organization's vision, why should
   anyone else be?

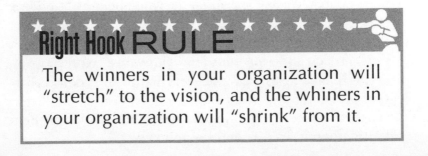

Right Hook RULE

The winners in your organization will
"stretch" to the vision, and the whiners in
your organization will "shrink" from it.

TKO Tale

Once a year in October, I conduct a 3-day Strategy Summit in Las Vegas. It's an intensive workshop during which attendees spend 3 days planning the next year's vision, strategy, and tactics. After they leave the workshop they have several assignments to complete and fax to my office: meetings to hold, tasks to distribute, strategies to prioritize, and the like. After all the time, expense, and effort our clients invest in fulfilling their leadership obligations to create the organizations' vision, I still see some of their efforts fall short because they fail to heed some of the pitfalls we discuss in the class. Following are several factors that can derail your vision efforts. It's been said that your biggest vulnerability is the one you're unaware of. If this is true, pay heed to these pitfalls so you can avoid or overcome them.

Left Jab Laws

1. People will not buy into your vision until they've bought into you as their manager.
2. Don't rush the process. You "crock-pot" the vision process, you don't "microwave" it.

You're not going to devise a meaningful vision and strategy in one 45-minute meeting. Remember, at my seminar in Las Vegas we spend 3 intensive days on the subject and then the attendees have several weeks worth of follow-up tasks and assignments to complete in order to position themselves to successfully roll out the vision and earn the buy-in from their teams.

3. Don't allow people to reduce the vision to their comfort zone.

Your job is to stretch people to your vision and not allow them to shrink you down to their level of thinking.

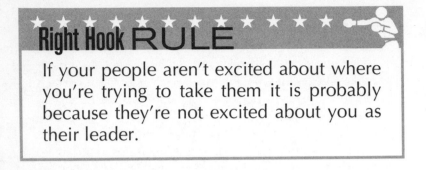

Right Hook RULE

If your people aren't excited about where you're trying to take them it is probably because they're not excited about you as their leader.

4. Realize that not everyone will be willing to make the trip. A bold vision and innovative strategy for reaching it will flush out those who are just along for the ride.

When I was a young leader I was so naïve. I thought that everyone wanted to grow and reach their potential. I eventually discovered that some folks want to be left alone. They don't see what all the fuss is about concerning "stretching" and "vision." They're quite content to stay where they are and begin living defensively. This is one of the saddest realizations a leader makes. But it is not your job to hit people in the head with a bat and drag them around the bases. It

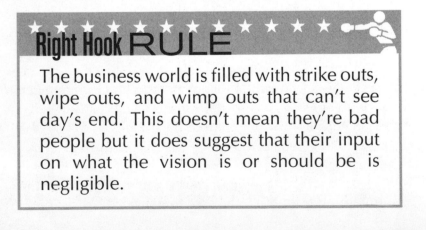

Right Hook RULE

The business world is filled with strike outs, wipe outs, and wimp outs that can't see day's end. This doesn't mean they're bad people but it does suggest that their input on what the vision is or should be is negligible.

should not be too much to expect them to want to make the trip. Sometimes an organization will outgrow some of its people. At one time they were solid contributors, but the organization grew and they didn't. As I pointed out previously, you can't allow the people who refuse to stoke the vision flames to soak them instead.

5. Not being clear or uncomplicated in the vision and its strategy for getting there is a common pitfall.

At my Strategy Summit I recommend that attendees limit their vision to three measurable components. The vision doesn't have to contain three elements, but it should not exceed that amount. Three is memorable; it is manageable, you can more easily track it and communicate it. Not everyone pays heed to this advice. A client once approached me with his eight-page vision and strategy for the year. It was overwhelming. I felt sorry for him because he had put a lot of work into it. But his vision was useless. If we were able to shrink the eight pages down and put it on two-ply, unscented paper and attach it to a rest room wall it would have at least been able to serve some modest purpose. As it stood, the only function it could possibly serve was as kindling.

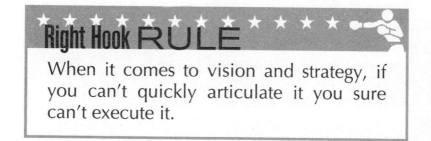

Right Hook RULE

When it comes to vision and strategy, if you can't quickly articulate it you sure can't execute it.

6. Start with a 1-year vision. Most people can't realistically see past a year.

It's fine to have 5- and 10-year plans if you're at the top of the organization, but the average frontline worker has trouble seeing past the next pay period, much less 5 years down the road.

Turn your vision into your annual campaign and introduce a new crusade each year.

7. Review progress often. Have regular Vision Meetings to review progress. This keeps the campaign at the forefront of everyone's mind.

If, during your review, you realize that your plan is not working, then change it! Don't fall in love with your plan! Lock like a laser on your goal but stay flexible in your approach to reaching it.

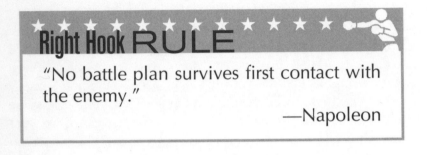

Right Hook RULE

"No battle plan survives first contact with the enemy."

—Napoleon

8. Expect to pay a price. A vision that doesn't cost you something is just a daydream.

The vision process will cost you plenty: time, money, energy, and other resources. But the prize is worth the price. In fact, if you ever get discouraged by what the vision seems to be costing you, weigh out the cost of being without direction, purpose, and inspiration throughout the workplace and you'll quickly realize that your efforts are worth the payoff in the end.

9. Expect resistance.

Remember, not everyone wants to grow and nearly everyone resists change. The good news is that once the vision catches on and you gain some short-term wins you will develop the momentum that starts to bring the doubters and stragglers along. Resistance sometimes comes in code. People don't come right out and say, "I don't want to change" or "I don't want to grow." Instead, they start saying and doing subtle things that undermine your efforts. Meet these actions head on and let the perpetrators know that the vision is not an experiment and that you'd like to make the trip with them, but will do so without them if necessary.

Right Hook RULE

Nothing silences cynics like results!

10. Stop waiting for the perfect time to begin. There is no perfect time so you may as well get started. Procrastination is compromising your future.

If you're halfway through the year, I don't recommend you wait until next year to begin. Instead, devise a second-half vision to convert the final 6 months of the year into a bold campaign.

11.Be sure that the influencers are on board first.

Any organizational change effort is dead unless the influencers get on board early. Regardless of how effective you are as a manager, you cannot do it alone. Meet privately with your key influencers for their input and support. These people will become advocates who help you spread the vision epidemic and cause it to cascade throughout the rank and file. If you fail to convert the influencers into advocates they tend to become saboteurs. In that case, you have only one choice and that is to replace them.

Right Hook RULE

There is not one *right* or *wrong* way to go about setting and working toward a vision for your organization. Use these ideas as a framework and a guide. Stay flexible and make it work for you.

Nine Quick Reminders for the Journey

1. Always set visions in terms of what you want, not what you want to avoid.

2. Somewhere along the line the manager has to move away from consensus and democracy and make the hard decisions as to exactly what the vision should be.

3. Everyone in the organization should understand what's in it for them—as well as the organization.

4. Constant communication is the key to building credibility that the vision is for real and in creating focus toward the plan for getting there.

5. Review progress often. Have Vision Meetings and, as time goes on, add more people from diverse areas of your operation to the meetings. The key is inclusion, not exclusion.

6. Continue to stretch and refine your vision as you reach different aspects of it. Make it an endless process of renewal.

7. Make the vision easy to understand. After a short while, everyone in your organization should be able to articulate what it is and why it's important.

8. Suggested areas to include in your vision are—but certainly not limited to—total sales and profit, percentage increases, market share, customer service rankings, national sales rankings, and so forth.

9. This is hard work. There are no shortcuts. Take your time and do it right. Expect resistance. Pay the price. The rewards are incredible.

The Vital Role of Strategy

As important as vision is to your organization it is only the beginning. You still need a strategy to help you reach your goals. In my book, *Up Your Business: 7 Steps to Fix, Build, or Stretch*

Your Organization (Wiley, 2003), I discuss strategy at length. In chapter four, *"It's All Right to Aim High if You Have Plenty of Ammo"* I outline a handful of the key precepts of strategy in the following points.

Vision without strategy is hallucination.

Left Jab Laws

1. Strategies change often. Remain focused on your goal without becoming attached to how you get there. If you're falling short of desired outcomes don't lower the goal; change the plan.

2. Determine the highest-value strategic targets—those that will bring the fastest and most substantial return—and hit them simultaneously. By hitting several key areas at once, you give the system less opportunity to bounce back and reestablish the status quo. Thus, your change is more likely to become embedded in your culture.

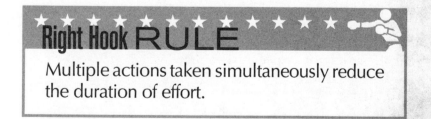

Multiple actions taken simultaneously reduce the duration of effort.

3. If you are working longer and harder but are still not seeing results it is an indication that you are locked in a tactical struggle and must step back and reevaluate your strategic

targets to ensure they are the right ones. You are most likely hitting the wrong targets and must change your approach.

4. Keep your strategies simple. The fewer steps the better and the more flat your command structure, the faster you can move.

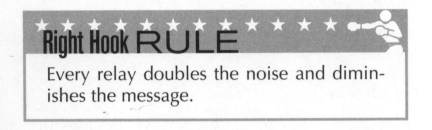

Right Hook RULE

Every relay doubles the noise and diminishes the message.

5. It is not the leader's job to create the entire strategy alone. The leader's role is to create the context for others to contribute to the content of the strategy. This gives you ideas that you wouldn't have thought of on your own and offers the employees a sense of ownership in the process that they would not have gained if they were merely carrying out your dictated orders.

6. In times of crisis it is imperative that the manager become more decisive in devising strategies and in doing so without taking the time to gain consensus, if necessary.

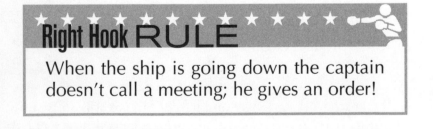

Right Hook RULE

When the ship is going down the captain doesn't call a meeting; he gives an order!

Standing Eight-Count Questions

1. If ten people in your organization were asked to write down their visions without conferring with one another would their answers be identical?

2. Overall, do your employees feel like they are building a dike to save a city or are they filling sandbags with dirt?

3. Once you create a vision, how will you keep it alive 4, 6, 8, and 10 months down the line?

4. Who in your organization are likely to be the most passionate vision advocates?

5. Who in your organization are most likely to resist the change involved with vision?

6. If you've had organizational visions in the past, have they been large enough so that initially you weren't sure how you'd get there?

7. What are your three key strategies for growing your business?

8. Do you normally change a faulty plan fast enough?

Notes

ROUND 8

Hold People
Accountable
for Results

Opening Bell

I love going on cruise ship vacations and recently I took my second trip to Alaska. Life is so safe on a cruise. You don't have to do anything in particular and there are no deadlines to meet. You can eat ten times per day if you like. The result of being so "safe" and comfortable on my last cruise was that I gained 7 pounds in 7 days. My wife told me that if I got any fatter, I could return home and run for sheriff! This scenario reminded me about how it is in business as well: Human beings aren't at their best when life is too safe. They get rusty, lazy, and complacent, and then they lose their edge. We need the positive stress of deadlines and urgency in order to bring out our best. These important components of a workplace environment start with having expectations that are both clear and high enough.

If you do not hold employees accountable for results you will lose your influence as their manager. When you fail to deal effectively with poor-performing employees you will lose the esteem of your best performers. Needless to say, if you want to be an effective leader of people you must perform these necessary, but oftentimes unpleasant, parts of your job, with finesse, speed, decisiveness, and courage.

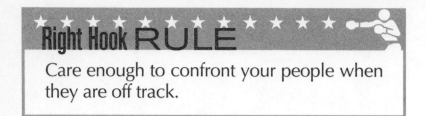

Right Hook RULE

Care enough to confront your people when they are off track.

The Two Big Problems with Accountability

Without a doubt, holding people accountable is much more difficult if you haven't established performance and behavioral expectations in the first place. In fact, there are two major problems organizations have when they do set expectations: normally they are neither clear enough nor high enough. So, first things first: You must set expectations and hold people accountable; but you must also ensure that they are crystal clear—and in writing—and they are high enough to stretch people because, ultimately, your performance and behavioral expectations define your culture.

Two Quick Tips When Setting Expectations

1. Make certain that what you expect is clear enough and that it is in writing. Don't assume people know what you want them to do. Your job as a leader is to create clarity. Once you've done this, you have a benchmark to hold others accountable, which also improves the level of performance in your workplace.

Right Hook RULE

Ambiguity is the enemy of accountability.

2. Ensure that your expectations are high enough. Low expectations are worse than no expectations because they make the wrong things official.

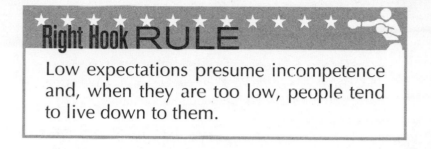

Low expectations presume incompetence and, when they are too low, people tend to live down to them.

Obviously, you can't set the bar so high that it overwhelms people but you can't leave it so low that they can just get by either. The art of leadership is finding that just-right place—the sweet spot—where people believe they can hit the target but they know that they won't be able to get there with business as usual. They will have to extend themselves, make some changes, and actually break a sweat.

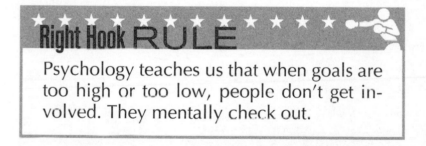

Psychology teaches us that when goals are too high or too low, people don't get involved. They mentally check out.

You do no one a favor by setting a soft set of expectations. You narrow their vision, shrink their thinking, and condition them to mediocrity until average becomes acceptable. But a high set of expectations for others must start with a high set of expectations for yourself. There is no credibility if you raise another's bar but yours is so low that you keep tripping over it! And if you're going to raise the bar, you'll need to train your people and give them the coaching they need in order to hit the mark. After all, if all your people have ever done is run around the block and you're going to ask them to run a marathon, you'll need to get them ready.

TKO Tale

What holding people accountable is all about is oftentimes misunderstood by leaders at all levels. This point was brought home to me while I was speaking in a foreign country to a group of professional and highly developed leaders in the automotive industry. My topic concerned accountability. After offering several tips for holding others accountable and confronting nonperformers an attendee in the back of the room raised his hand and asked, "Holding others accountable, caring enough to confront them, and imposing consequences for those failing to perform probably works just fine in the States. But over here we're gentlemen. How do you recommend that we handle these situations?"

I replied that holding people accountable doesn't imply that you have to be mean, disrespectful, insulting, or an outright jerk. In fact, it's much more effective if you don't stoop to this approach. Holding people accountable means that you're clear about where you stand and where they stand; you are direct, firm, and fair.

Right Hook RULE

Holding others accountable is not at odds with also being courteous and respectful.

Six Keys to Accountability

1. Clearly define what you expect up front and put these expectations in writing.

Without this simple discipline, the question becomes, "accountable for what?" You have an obligation to define what you expect both in terms of behaviors and technical job tasks.

Effective managers do not let people live in a gray area. They clearly establish where both they and their people stand. My book, *If You Don't Make Waves, You'll Drown: 10 Hard-Charging Strategies for Leading in Politically Correct Times* (Wiley, 2005) outlines 25 sample expectations in chapter one. Based on the feedback, it's been one of the most helpful sections of the book.

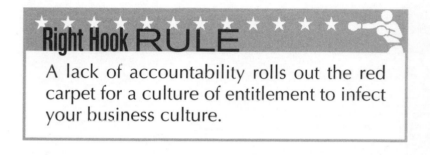

Right Hook RULE

A lack of accountability rolls out the red carpet for a culture of entitlement to infect your business culture.

2. Redefine what you expect from time to time.
Expectations can oftentimes become cloudy, watered down, or conveniently forgotten. It's essential that you not only tirelessly communicate what you expect but that you also redefine your expectations as needed.

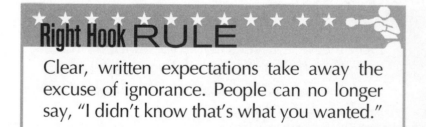

Right Hook RULE

Clear, written expectations take away the excuse of ignorance. People can no longer say, "I didn't know that's what you wanted."

3. Holding people accountable means that consequences for failing to perform are imposed.
A law of behavioral science indicates that if you want to change a behavior you must change the consequences for that behavior.

The consequence is the "or else." And, sometimes in management, it comes down to issuing "or elses." "Be on time, or else," "Hit this number, or else," and the like. Too many leaders give endless pep talks, issue empty threats, and, as a result, are mocked by their people behind their backs. Consequences are the teeth necessary to protect and reinforce your high-performance business culture and your personal credibility as a manager.

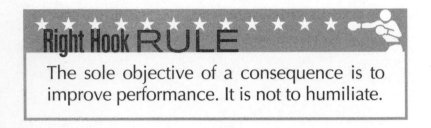

Right Hook RULE

The sole objective of a consequence is to improve performance. It is not to humiliate.

4. Holding people accountable means that you give them fast and honest feedback on their performances.
If people are great, tell them. On the other hand, if they're failing, tell them that as well but don't just leave them there. Help them devise a plan to turn things around.

Right Hook RULE

Don't let employees continue in their errant ways to the point that their bad habits and behaviors are so engrained that they become incorrigible.

5. Holding people accountable is nothing to apologize for.
Allowing someone to live in a gray area where there are no absolutes—no winning or losing; no right or wrong; no success or failure—*is* something to apologize for.

Temporary discomfort is better than temporary ease if it averts permanent failure.

6. When you fail to hold others accountable, you have chosen a strategy of surrender.

At this stage, you don't manage the employees, they manage you. They have managed to diminish your standards down to their level and lower your expectations to meet their performance. You're no longer stretching them, they're shrinking you!

Failing to hold employees accountable fosters a sense of "you owe me" that causes them to put in the minimum, expect the maximum in return, and begin to live in a state of denial that convinces them that they're doing the job when, in reality, they're merely taking up space and so begin to constipate productivity.

Standing Eight-Count Questions

1. Do you have written performance expectations for your employees?

2. Do you go over these during an interview upon hiring, and review them as well during one-on-ones?

3. Have you established behavioral expectations (core values) that define the behaviors that mean the most to your organization and on which you are unwilling to compromise?

4. When is the last time you redefined expectations in your organization? Is it time to do so?

5. When you hold people accountable do you attack the performance or the performer?

6. Are your expectations high enough so that your employees cannot reach them with a business-as-usual approach?

7. Do you believe that you may have set some expectations too high and that people have mentally checked out of ever trying to reach them?

8. Do you hold yourself to a high enough set of expectations and hold yourself accountable as an example to your team?

Notes

ROUND 9

Deal Effectively with Poor Performers

Opening Bell

I was so egotistical in my first management job that I felt for sure I could turn anyone's performance around if I worked with them long enough. I used to take it as a personal challenge to save employees and bring them up to speed. I also used compassion as an excuse to keep them employed. After all, some of them had been with us for years and had families to support. But not only did keeping the wrong people for too long diminish the rest of the team's morale, it made a laughing stock out of my own credibility. In fact, the number one question people would ask me after I would finally terminate a poor performer was, "what took you so long?" As I look back on my past behavior I realize one sobering truth: I really didn't keep these people for reasons of personal compassion but for reasons of personal convenience. Frankly, it was easier on me in the short run to keep working with what I had than to go out and recruit, interview, test, and train, with the thought that it might take months to get someone new up to speed. By keeping the wrong people for reasons of personal comfort rather than doing what was best for the rest of the team and for the organization overall, I became guilty of a form of embezzlement. Sadly, there are far too many embezzlers in management positions today and their reluctance or refusal to face the tough issues concerning poor performers puts the health of the entire organization at risk.

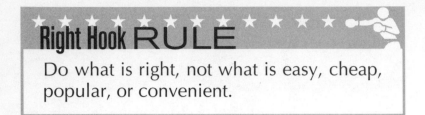

Right Hook RULE

Do what is right, not what is easy, cheap, popular, or convenient.

The Penalties of Poor Performance

Dealing with poor performers is not supposed to be easy. But making the tough calls is one of the expectations that separates you from the front-line personnel, and it is a big part of what you're being paid for. The best managers make smart choices concerning poor performers and they do so quickly. They realize that a leader who does not effectively handle these people will hurt the following:

1. The organization's ability to achieve its vision.

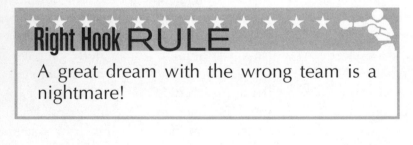

Right Hook RULE

A great dream with the wrong team is a nightmare!

2. The morale of top performers.

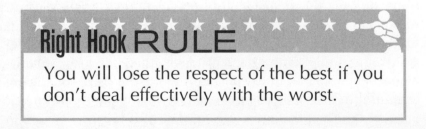

Right Hook RULE

You will lose the respect of the best if you don't deal effectively with the worst.

3. Their own credibility.

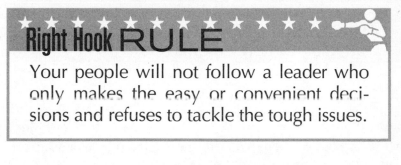

Right Hook RULE

Your people will not follow a leader who only makes the easy or convenient decisions and refuses to tackle the tough issues.

4. The low performer's self-image and potential success.

Right Hook RULE

While terminating a poor performer may seem harsh, it is less harsh than allowing someone to remain in a position where they're failing, where they're losing their self esteem and have absolutely no chance whatsoever of reaching their potential as a human being.

Left Jab Laws

Apply the Three Ts:
From time to time it is helpful for leaders to ask themselves a very important question concerning everyone on their team: "Knowing what I now know about this person, if he or she applied for the job today, would I hire him or her?" In other words, knowing what I *now* know about good old Fred's attitude, work ethic, character, and production levels, if he came in today and applied, would I give him the job? If the answer is "yes," great! Go

on to the next name on your team and ask this question. This is an eye-opening exercise that helps you step back and honestly evaluate people whose mediocrity you may have become comfortable with or desensitized to. If, while asking this question, the answer you arrive at is "No! Are you kidding me? Knowing what I now know about him there is no way I'd rehire him!" then you have an unacceptable situation on your hands. Most of us could agree that having someone working for you that you wouldn't rehire again, if given the opportunity, constitutes a real problem. But it's not time to worry about fault. It's time to fix the problem. In order to do that you must evaluate your options for someone you wouldn't rehire. These options are known as the "Three Ts." In other words, your options for this unacceptable employee are to train them, transfer them, or terminate them. Please note that there are not four Ts—there is no "tolerate" them! Consider the following strategies concerning each of these three Ts:

1. Training: If low performance is due to poor or undeveloped skills, it calls for training. Before you fire an employee you make certain that you've done your job. Have you set clear expectations, trained the person, given them feedback, and learned how to motivate them?

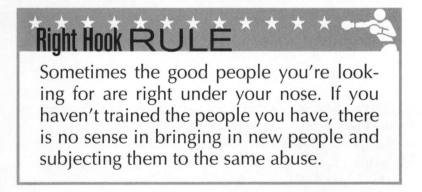

Right Hook RULE

Sometimes the good people you're looking for are right under your nose. If you haven't trained the people you have, there is no sense in bringing in new people and subjecting them to the same abuse.

2. Transfer: Sometimes an employee is a poor performer because he or she is expected to work in a job that does not

match his or her skills and talents. If the employee has a good attitude, solid character, a desire to succeed, and shares your values, he or she can be transferred to a position that matches his or her strengths. However, transfers are not an excuse to move a person around endlessly looking for his or her niche in life. Don't move someone around just to prolong the unpleasantness of firing him or her.

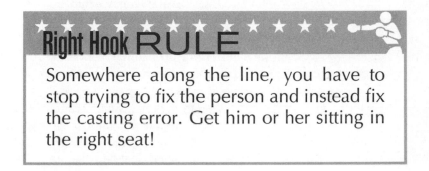

Right Hook RULE

Somewhere along the line, you have to stop trying to fix the person and instead fix the casting error. Get him or her sitting in the right seat!

3. Terminating: Terminating an employee can be one of the toughest decisions you will ever make. However, it is also one of the most important decisions you must make. Regardless of your personal feelings for someone, his or her own comfort cannot come before what is best for the team and the organization overall. Besides, you do no one a favor by allowing someone to remain in a position where he or she is failing. Life is too short! Free these people up to discover their potential elsewhere.

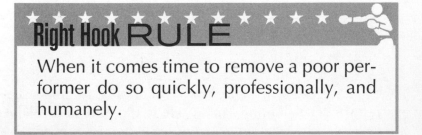

Right Hook RULE

When it comes time to remove a poor performer do so quickly, professionally, and humanely.

TKO Tale

In my seminars, I often ask if anyone has ever had to fire someone, just to have that person come back to them at some time and thank them for letting them go. Inevitably, some attendees raise their hands each time I ask this question.

I once fired an employee that had worked for me for a number of years and, in the course of that time, we had become good friends. I agonized over the decision and gave him six second chances but none of them made any difference. Nor did my speeches about how things had better improve. Finally, I decided that enough was enough and put my personal feelings aside and fired him. He was shocked. He left in a huff and I didn't' hear from him again for several years. I had just about forgotten about him when I received a call one day from "George," who told me the following:

"I hated you the day you fired me. I thought my life was ruined. I had to go tell my wife that I had lost my job and I knew that she'd doubt my ability to provide for her and our son. However, I found a job selling medical supplies and I loved it. Instead of waiting for people to come in and buy from me I was out calling on them and I discovered that this was what I was good at. In 2 years I had become the top salesperson in my region and in my third year in the business I became the number one salesperson in the country. I've held that title for 2 years. I'm making more money now and having more fun that I ever have had in my life. I called today to thank you for firing me. I couldn't see it at the time but now I know that it was the nudge I needed to discover what I was really supposed to be doing with my life."

1. Separate the performer from the performance.
Don't make it personal. We all have equal value as human beings but we don't all bring equal value to the workplace. Value and respect the person but confront his or her performance.

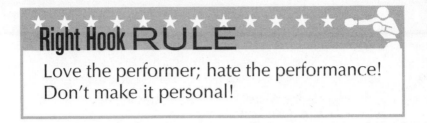

Right Hook RULE

Love the performer; hate the performance!
Don't make it personal!

2. Don't keep an obvious misfit merely because you'd be shorthanded if you let him or her go.

This is a common rationalization that I hear in nearly all of my seminars. Inevitably, an attendee will remark, "Dave, I'd like to get rid of so and so but I have no one to replace him. As a result, we'll be shorthanded and my good people will be overworked." The best way out of this situation is to become a more proactive recruiter so that you have a pipeline of employees lined up to work in your business and aren't held hostage by morons, misfits, or moochers. For more strategies on recruiting, read my books *TKO Hiring* (Wiley, 2007) and *Up Your Business* (Wiley, 2003).

Right Hook RULE

When you fire nonperformers your best workers may become temporarily overworked. However, if you force your top performers to work with incompetents or surround them with idiots, they're also overworked! Most people would rather be overworked carrying their own load rather than bearing their burden and someone else's.

3. The best way to prevent having to deal with poor performers is to stop hiring recklessly. If you're bringing people on

board who give you little or nothing to work with, then you're doomed from the outset.

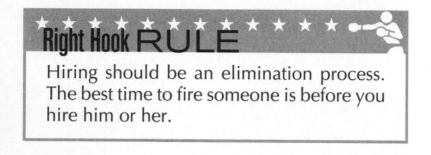

Hiring should be an elimination process. The best time to fire someone is before you hire him or her.

4. Sometimes the weak link on your team is a top performer who doesn't share your values. These people are just as dangerous and sometimes more so than the bottom dwellers. Their behavior creates distractions, breaks momentum, and publicly challenges the leader's highly esteemed values. When you tolerate dysfunctional behaviors from an employee just because they "hit their numbers" you're perceived as a sellout at best and a coward at worst.

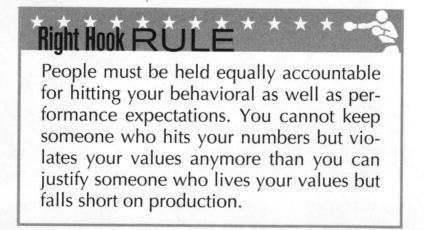

People must be held equally accountable for hitting your behavioral as well as performance expectations. You cannot keep someone who hits your numbers but violates your values anymore than you can justify someone who lives your values but falls short on production.

Standing Eight-Count Questions

1. Are your performance expectations high enough?
2. Do you have behavioral expectations and are they held sacred?
3. What are the consequences for those who fail to meet either set of expectations?
4. Do you have a weak link that performs well but doesn't live your values? How will you turn this around?
5. Do you have someone on your team that you could turn-around by spending more time training them?
6. Is there an employee with a good attitude, character, and energy that is failing because he or she is working outside of his or her strength zone? Is there a place you can transfer this person?
7. If you must fire an employee, will he or she have seen it coming or will you catch him or her by surprise?
8. When you confront poor performers, do you have the discipline and demeanor to be firm, respectful, and professional?

Notes

ROUND 10

Knockout Summary for Follow-Through

Let's conclude with a Knockout summary of major points from each Round. All Round summaries will include key points included in that Round and an occasional question to help you evaluate your progress. Review these notes often as a catalyst to consistent action. This is the most important strategy of all because if you fail to follow through, you fail.

★ ★ ★ ★ ★ ★ ★ ★ ★ ★ ★ ★ ★ ★

Right Hook RULE

The biggest gap in business is the gap between knowing and doing. To elevate your organization, you must develop the discipline to close this gap.

1. Does your management style reflect one who spends more time charting results or charting the course? Do you change quickly and before you have to or do you spend more time defending the status quo? Most importantly, do you maintain your people and organization or do you stretch them?

2. Does your workplace environment have high-enough expectations? Is it vision-driven? Are you visible and accessible enough to create the right tone for your environment?

3. Do you know what motivates each member of your team and do you customize your personal style to fit each person? Do you give enough feedback on performance? Do you schedule one-on-ones with your people? Is your training consistent and credible?

4. If each of your people were asked what the vision for their organization is for the year, would all of their answers be identical? Can you list your three key strategies for reaching your vision? If not, do you know what they should be?

5. Are your expectations for performance and behaviors in writing? Do your people clearly understand them? Do you have people working for you that you wouldn't rehire? Which of the Three Ts best applies to each of these people?

Right Hook RULE

Life rewards action! It doesn't reward experience, wisdom, or knowledge. Get up off your knowledge and do something!

TKO Summary

Round One: Look in the Mirror

1. Focus on the things you can control and stop getting distracted by those that you cannot control.

2. Continue to upgrade your own skills because you can't export to others what you don't have, and you can't take them on a journey that you haven't been on.

3. Look in the mirror because your team is a reflection of you. Their speed will mirror your speed.

Round Two: Understand the Truth about Titles

1. A title doesn't make you a manager. It simply gives you a chance to become one.
2. Leadership is performance and not position.
3. People must buy into you before they buy into where you're trying to take them.
4. If you cannot influence people you cannot lead them.
5. Remember that many people without official titles are leaders. They have influence and get results.
6. It is your job to establish relationships with your followers. It is not their job to chase you down and connect with you.

Round Three: Balance Solid Management Skill with Strong Leadership Ability

1. Leave your people better than you found them. Impact them! Don't just maintain them.
2. Lead from the front. Don't just preside in your office chair. Chart the course, not just the results.
3. Change before you have to. Don't wait for the bottom to fall out. Fix the roof while the sun is shining.
4. When you have to make a change, do so quickly. The longer you look at it the tougher it gets.
5. Work through the discomfort and pain of change when it arises or you won't grow.
6. Don't become so immersed in administrivia that you begin to overmanage and underlead.
7. Make yourself more visible and accessible to your followers.
8. Remember that to lead means to get out front and act as a catalyst.

Round Four: Create a Winning Workplace Environment

1. Act as an organizational thermostat, not a thermometer.
2. You can't create the right environment by memo, voicemail, or e-mail. Don't talk like a leader and then act like an anchor.
3. Set expectations that are clear enough and high enough. This is a key to accountability.
4. Make sure your organization is vision driven because vision-driven organizations feel differently. There is more purpose, teamwork, and urgency. Follow the steps in Round seven for making this happen.
5. Publicly control your attitude and emotions because as a leader you are always on display.
6. When you make a mistake, come clean quick and teach others to do the same.

Round Five: Become a Powerful Motivator

1. Take the human capital you've been entrusted with and make it more valuable tomorrow than it is today.
2. Create an environment that is motivating by removing potential demotivators from the workplace.
3. Address internal motivational needs so that the external rewards have a greater impact.
4. Customize your motivational approach to fit each of your people. You must know them to move them.
5. Motivations change over time so it's essential that you stay in touch with what motivates your people.
6. Do what you say you'll do, when you say you'll do it, and how you say you'll do it. Make certain that your words and deeds are consistent.
7. Increase positive reinforcement. Be fast, specific, and consistent.

Round Six: Train and Coach Your People to Reach Their Fullest Potential

1. Make training meetings one of the nonnegotiable disciplines in your organization.
2. Find ways to get people involved during the meetings.
3. Don't just talk about what good performance looks like; show people what it looks like!
4. Make training meetings credible. Top managers should attend.
5. Schedule and conduct meaningful one-on-one coaching sessions to develop your people.
6. Follow the ask, listen, coach, reinforce, and challenge process.
7. Compile a one-on-one binder.

Round Seven: Create a Dynamic Vision and Strategy for Your Organization

1. Vision is the manager's responsibility. You cannot delegate organizational direction.
2. Vision should be big enough so that initially, you're not quite sure how you'll get there. You should not be able to reach a vision with a business-as-usual approach.
3. Effective visions cause you to do something each day that you wouldn't otherwise do without them.
4. The five Cs for the vision process involve: catching, casting, communicating constantly until there is a genuine commitment to reach it.
5. People must participate in the strategy process. They will support what they help create.
6. Avoid the eleven listed pitfalls that will derail your vision. Your biggest vulnerability is the one you're unaware of so review these points often.
7. Vision without strategy is hallucination.
8. Strategies change often. Don't fall in love with your plan.

9. Determine strategic targets and hit them simultaneously because multiple actions taken at the same time reduce the duration of effort.

10. If you work longer and harder but do not progress it indicates you are locked in a tactical struggle and must reevaluate and hit new targets.

11. The manager's job is to create the context for others to contribute to the content of the strategy.

12. Tough times call for more decisiveness from the manager. You may have to stop making suggestions and start giving orders.

Round Eight: Hold People Accountable for Results

1. Clearly define performance and behavioral expectations because ambiguity is the enemy of accountability.

2. When you don't hold people accountable you lose your influence as a leader.

3. Redefine what you expect from time to time.

4. When people fail to perform, apply consequences as necessary.

5. Part of holding others accountable means you give them feedback to keep them out of a gray area.

6. Holding people accountable is nothing to apologize for.

7. Holding people accountable doesn't mean you must be harsh, mean, or disrespectful.

Round Nine: Deal Effectively with Poor Performers

1. If you would not rehire an employee you must apply one of the Three Ts.

2. The Three Ts are: train, transfer, or terminate.

3. When you don't remove a poor performer you lose the respect of your best people and put the interests of one person ahead of the good of the team.

4. You do no one a favor by allowing people to remain in a position where they're failing and cannot reach their potential as a human being.

5. We all have equal value as human beings but we don't all bring equal value to the workplace.

6. Love the performer, hate the performance.

7. Care enough to confront people when they're off track.

8. Don't hide behind personal compassion as a reason for failing to deal with a nonperformer when the truth is that you're keeping him or her for reasons of personal convenience.

Notes

Bibliography

Anderson, Dave. 2003. *Up Your Business.* Hoboken, NJ: Wiley.

Anderson, Dave. 2005. *If You Don't Make Waves You'll Drown.* Hoboken, NJ: Wiley.

Axelrod, Alan. 1999. *Patton on Leadership.* Paramus, NJ: Prentice Hall.

Maxwell, John C. 1998. *The 21 Irrefutable Laws of Leadership.* Nashville, TN: Thomas Nelson.

Phillips, Donald T. 1992. *Lincoln on Leadership.* New York: Warner.

Index